WYOMING
impressions

photography by Fred Pflughoft

Above: Lupine blossoms beneath Warbonnet Peak.
Facing page: Red Canyon near Lander.
Title page: In the Gros Ventre Mountains.
Front cover: White Rock and Squaretop Mountain reflected in the Green River.
Back cover: Devils Tower.

Photographs by John L. Hinderman appear on pages 26, 56, 58

ISBN 10: 1-56037-197-8
ISBN 13: 978-1-56037-197-7

© 2001 by Farcountry Press
Photography © 2001 by Fred Pflughoft

For more information about our books, write Farcountry Press, P.O. Box 5630, Helena, MT 59604; call (800) 821-3874; or visit www.farcountrypress.com.

Created, produced, and designed in the United States.
Printed in Korea.

16 15 14 13 12 11   3 4 5 6 7 8

Left: Lake Marie in the Snowy Range.

Below: Sunrise warms sturdy survivors beneath Heart Mountain near Cody.

Below the Beartooth Mountains, Island Lake basks in August sunlight.

Facing page: Pinnacle Buttes are part of the Absaroka Mountains.

A sunset view of Shell Canyon, Bighorn National Forest.

Left: Wind power in Sublette County.

Bison enjoy the warmth of Yellowstone National Park's Lower Geyser Basin in spring.

Facing page: In the Wyoming Range.

Chapel of the Transfiguration, an Episcopalian Church, was built in Grand Teton National Park in 1925.

Facing page: Sinks Canyon State Park near Lander.

Jack Frost has been at play in Grand Teton National Park, near Gros Ventre Junction.

Right; Mount Moran, at 12,605 feet, is the fourth highest peak in the Tetons.

Left: The Red Hills rise from the Gros Ventre River.

Ready for whatever comes along on the range.

Hoarfrost encases sagebrush in Seedskadee National Wildlife Refuge.

Facing page: Winter glow on Sweetwater County's Pine Canyon.

Beartooth Lake reflections—or alien landing craft?

Facing page: Stormy weather heads in over Keyhole State Park.

Facing page: Wind-drawn patterns mark Killpecker Dunes, Sweetwater County.

Trail Town's historic buildings and exhibits were reassembled on the original site of Cody.

Crawfish Creek in Yellowstone drops over Moose Falls.

Left: Winter magic at the Tetons.

Wolves, successfully reintroduced into Yellowstone National Park, are seldom seen by visitors.

Right: Granite Creek meanders out of the Gros Ventre Mountains.

Pond lilies grace the waters of Grand Teton.

Left: Bridger-Teton National Forest, touched with autumn gold.

Proud beauties near Story.

Facing page: Vedauwoo Rocks put a spell on Medicine Bow National Forest.

Left: Spring's bright colors soften the stern look of Flat Top Mountain.

Haying can be a quiet, almost restful activity—if done right.

Late spring and early summer bring a bright mosaic of wildflowers into bloom.

Facing page: Like a rocky sentinel, Devils Tower rises above the surrounding grassland and Ponderosa pine forests. Scientists aren't sure how this remarkable geologic formation came about, but it is believed to be a stock—a small intrusive body formed by magma that cooled underground and was later exposed by erosion.

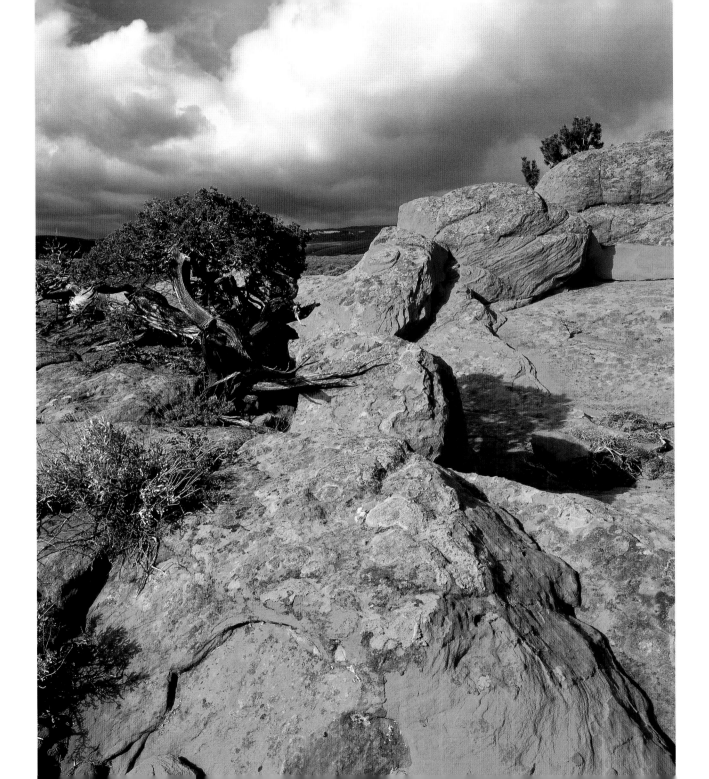

Lichen and wildflowers adorn a Medicine Bow National Forest rock outcrop.

Facing page: A natural rock fortress in Red Canyon.

Proper flyfishing attire, Wyoming style.

Right: Alcova Reservoir serves Casper.

Blue columbine.

Cirque of the Towers in Popo Agie Wilderness Area.

A mystic mood for Shoshone National Forest's Beartooth Lake.

Facing page: Packing into the Wind River Range through Upper Titcomb Basin.

One-stop service in Farson.

Left: Sunset silhouette of Mount Moran.

Lower Falls of the Yellowstone River, as seen from Lookout Point in Yellowstone National Park, is one of the park's heart-stopping views.

Right: A new day dawns at Keyhole State Park.

For its second career, a retired wagon wheel at Aladdin works as a trellis.

Left: Whitetailed deer make their getaway along the Belle Fourche River near Hulett.

Facing page: Castle Gardens Scenic Area near the town of Ten Sleep.

A backcountry powder hound enjoys Fortification Mountain in Bridger-Teton National Forest.

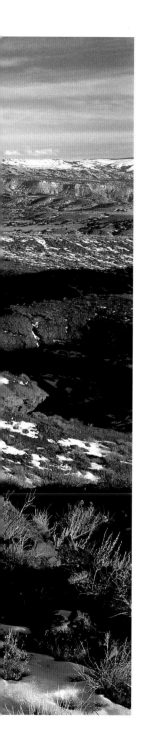

This old freight wagon is among exhibits at reconstructed Fort Caspar, near Casper.

Left: Wind-and-water sculpture above Bighorn Canyon National Recreation Area's Horseshoe Bend.

Rainbow Terrace in Hot Springs State Park, Thermopolis.

Right: Old Faithful Geyser and its namesake inn, Yellowstone National Park.

Moose, largest members of the deer family, love to dine on creek-bottom plants.

Right: Aspens glow during bright, cool autumn days in the Wind River Range.

Colorful huckleberry bushes, picked clean, perhaps by humans, perhaps by bears.

Facing page: Castle Geyser in Yellowstone's Upper Geyser Basin.

Fort Caspar, now reconstructed, was named for Caspar Collins, a young officer killed in an 1865 Indian battle nearby.

Right: Flaming Gorge National Recreation Area.

Facing page: Ice-cold water in the Snowy Range.

Bighorn Mountain foothills.

Right: The fantastic shape of Plume Rock stands near Farson.

South Pass City State Historic Site commemorates a stage station turned gold camp in 1867.

This fossilized turtle can be found at Wyoming Dinosaur Center in Thermopolis.

Left: East Temple Peak (to left) and Temple Peak (to right) peer down on Deep Lake in the Wind Rivers.

Right: West Thumb Geyser Basin is right at the edge of Yellowstone Lake, in the national park.

American white pelicans enjoy Wyoming's share of the Snake River.

In Grand Teton National Park, Cascade Creek tumbles through its own canyon.

Left: Trout Creek wends its way slowly across Yellowstone National Park's Hayden Valley.

A bull elk feeds along Yellowstone Lake.

Left: The Tetons from Schwabacher's Landing, Grand Teton National Park.

Red sky at morning, Yellowstone Lake sailors take warning..

Facing page: The badlands near Marbleton in winter garb.

Wyoming is one of the United States' leading oil producers, from derricks like this one near Powell.

Left: Boar's Tusk, viewed from Killpecker Dunes Wilderness Study Area.

Remembering the hardships and dreams of wagon train emigrants.

Right: Haying time on the North Platte River.

Fred Pflughoft turned from watercolor painting to landscape photography in 1988. His full-color photography appears regularly in regional and national periodicals, on calendars and postcards from United States and Canadian publishers, and is featured in the Farcountry Press books *Wyoming Wild and Beautiful*, *Oregon Wild and Beautiful*, *Yellowstone Wild and Beautiful*, *Grand Teton Wild and Beautiful*, and *Wyoming's Historic Forts*. He and his wife, Sue, have twin sons who join them in outdoor activities the year around.